Space Stations

by Martha E. H. Rustad

Consulting Editor: Gail Saunders-Smith, PhD

Consultant: Ilia Iankov Roussev, PhD
Associate Astronomer & Associate Professor
Institute for Astronomy, University of Hawaii at Manoa

SOUTH HUNTINGTON PUB. LIB.
145 PIDGEON HILL ROAD
HUNTINGTON STA., NY 11746

CAPSTONE PRESS
a capstone imprint

Pebble Plus is published by Capstone Press,
1710 Roe Crest Drive, North Mankato, Minnesota 56003.
www.capstonepub.com

Copyright © 2012 by Capstone Press, a Capstone imprint. All rights reserved.
No part of this publication may be reproduced in whole or in part, or stored in a retrieval system, or transmitted in any form or by any means, electronic, mechanical, photocopying, recording, or otherwise, without written permission of the publisher. For information regarding permission, write to Capstone Press,
1710 Roe Crest Drive, North Mankato, Minnesota 56003.

Library of Congress Cataloging-in-Publication Data
Rustad, Martha E. H. (Martha Elizabeth Hillman), 1975–
 Space stations / by Martha E. H. Rustad.
   p. cm.—(Pebble plus. exploring space)
 Includes bibliographical references and index.
 Summary: "Full-color photographs and simple text provide a brief introduction to space stations"—Provided by publisher.
 ISBN 978-1-4296-7579-6 (library binding)
 ISBN 978-1-4296-7895-7 (paperback)
 1. Space stations—Juvenile literature. I. Title.
 TL797.15.R87 2012
 629.44'2—dc23   2011021646

Editorial Credits
Erika Shores, editor; Alison Thiele, designer; Kathy McColley, production specialist

Photo Credits
NASA, cover, 1, 5, 7, 9, 11, 13, 15, 17, 19, 21

Artistic Effects
Shutterstock: glossygirl21, Primož Cigler, SmallAtomWorks

Note to Parents and Teachers

The Exploring Space series supports national science standards related to earth science. This book describes and illustrates space stations. The images support early readers in understanding the text. The repetition of words and phrases helps early readers learn new words. This book also introduces early readers to subject-specific vocabulary words, which are defined in the Glossary section. Early readers may need assistance to read some words and to use the Table of Contents, Glossary, Read More, Internet Sites, and Index sections of the book.

Printed in the United States of America in Stevens Point, Wisconsin.
082013   007677R

Table of Contents

What Is a Space Station?..... 4
Astronauts and Scientists..... 10
International Space Station ... 16
Future Space Travel......... 20

Glossary 22
Read More 23
Internet Sites.............. 23
Index 24

What Is a Space Station?

A space station floats high above Earth. Astronauts live and work inside this amazing laboratory.

Scientists plan space stations on Earth. Spacecraft carry up sections of the space station.

Astronauts use robots to put space stations together in space. Solar panels turn sunlight into energy for the station.

solar panels

Astronauts and Scientists

Astronauts live, work, eat,

and sleep in space stations.

Everything floats in space.

Astronauts sleep in bags

tied to the walls.

The crew works together
to build and fix the station.
They put on space suits
and go on space walks.

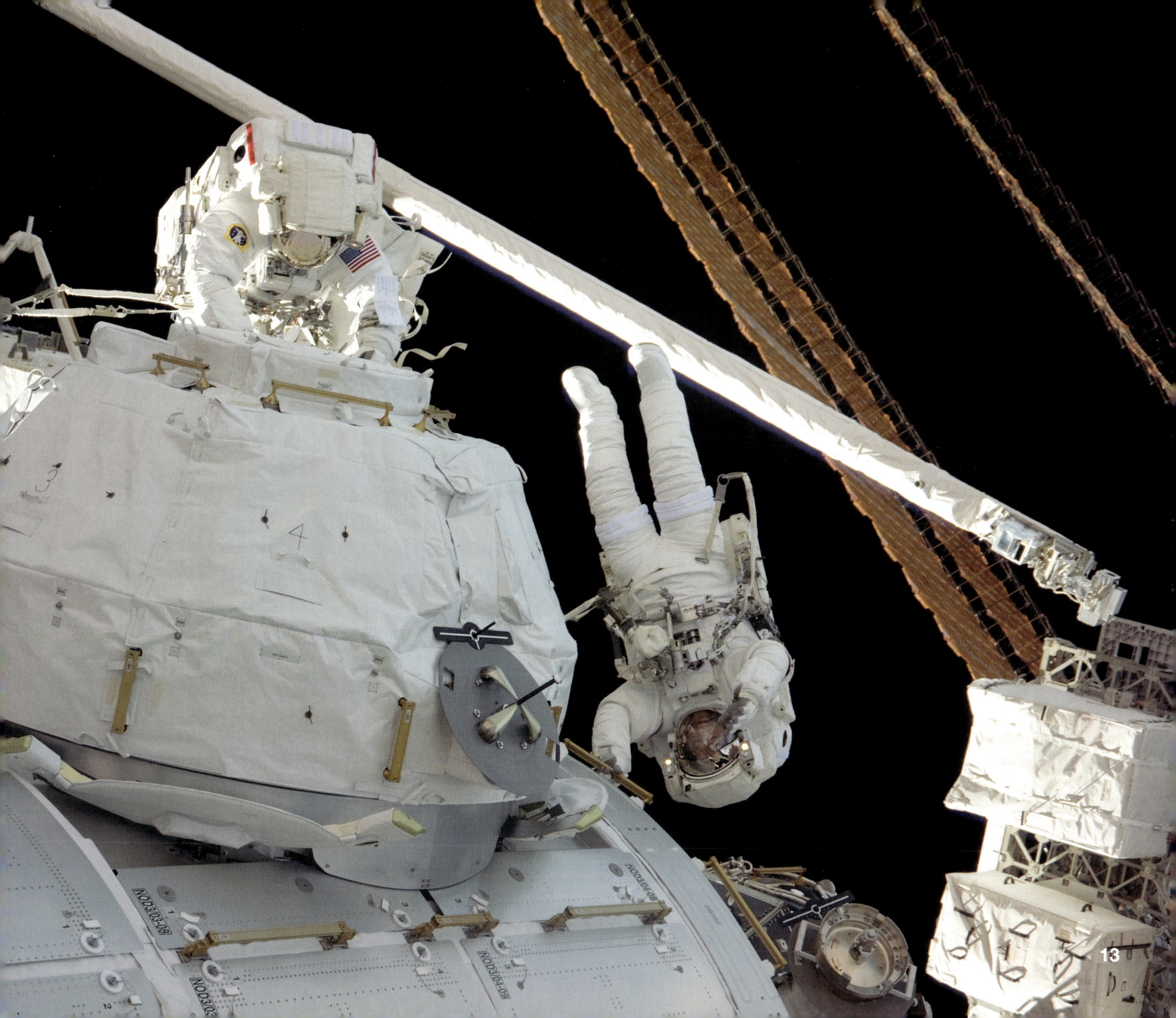

Astronauts study the stars and planets. They study how plants grow in space. Scientists on Earth study how space affects astronauts' bodies.

International Space Station

Many countries worked together to build the *International Space Station*. In 1998, the first parts blasted off into space.

The station was finished in 2011.

The *International Space Station* is as long as a football field. The station floats about 220 miles (354 kilometers) above Earth. It circles Earth once every 90 minutes.

Future Space Travel

In the future, a space station may be like a train station. Astronauts might stop there on their way to another planet.

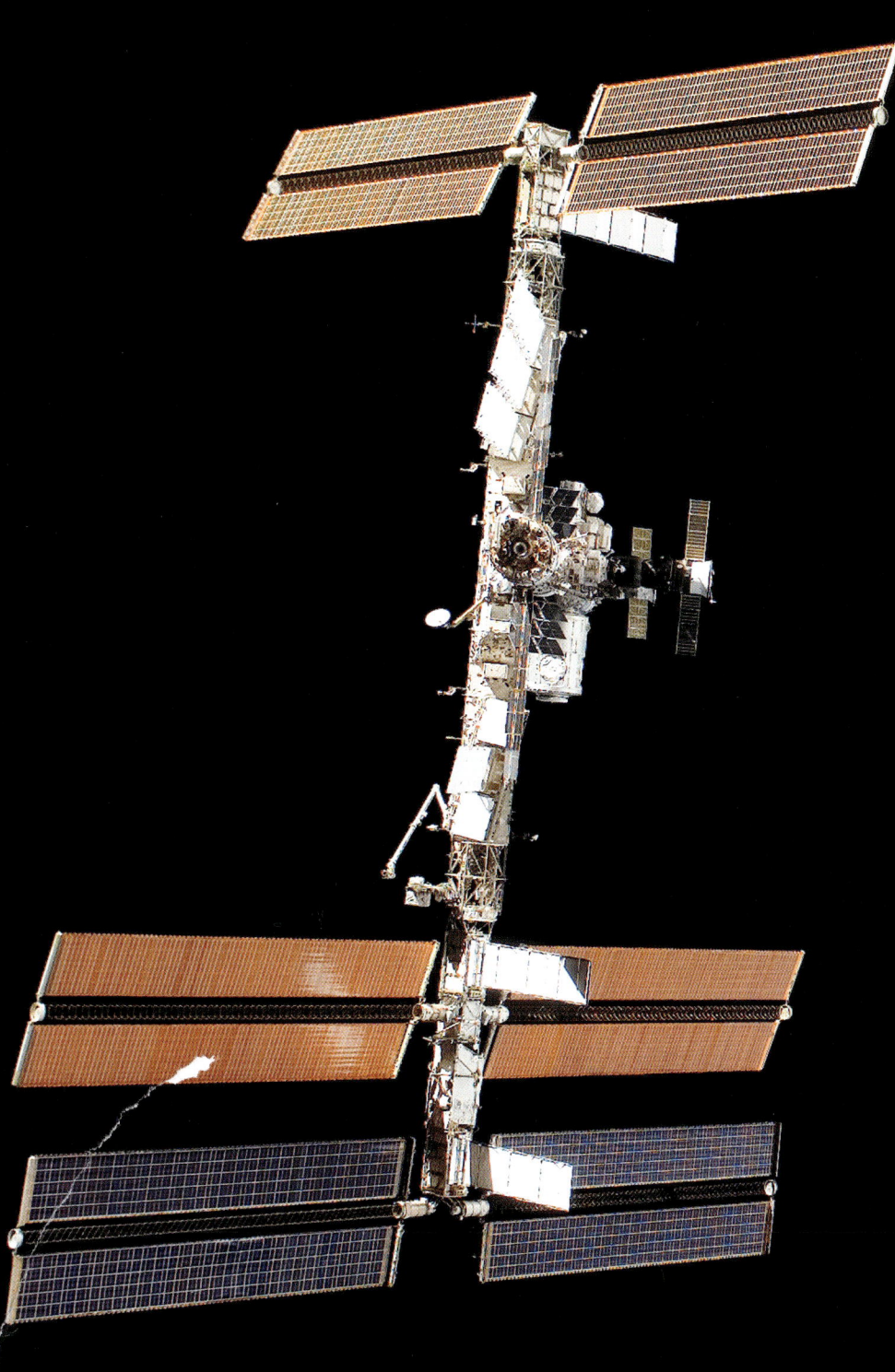

Glossary

astronaut—a person who is trained to live and work in space

laboratory—a room or building with equipment for scientific experiments

planet—a large object that orbits a star

solar panel—a flat surface that collects sunlight and turns it into power

spacecraft—a vehicle that travels into space

Read More

Braun, Eric. *If I Were an Astronaut.* Dream Big! Minneapolis: Picture Window Books, 2010.

Gross, Miriam J. *All about Space Stations.* Blast Off! New York: PowerKids Press, 2009.

Kortenkamp, Steve. *Space Stations.* The Solar System. Mankato, Minn.: Capstone Press, 2008.

Internet Sites

FactHound offers a safe, fun way to find Internet sites related to this book. All of the sites on FactHound have been researched by our staff.

Here's all you do:

Visit *www.facthound.com*

Type in this code: 9781429675796

Index

astronauts, 4, 8, 10, 14, 20
building, 8, 12, 16
Earth, 4, 6, 14, 18
International Space Station, 16, 18
planets, 14, 20
planning, 6
robots, 8

scientists, 6, 14
size, 18
solar panels, 8
spacecraft, 6
space suits, 12
space walks, 12
stars, 14
studying, 14

Word Count: 186
Grade: 1
Early-Intervention Level: 21